CATCHING THEIR TALK IN A BOX

the *Life-Story* of
JOY RIDDERHOF

by
Betty M. Hockett

GEORGE FOX PRESS
(a Barclay Press imprint)

BARCLAY PRESS

211 N. MERIDIAN ST., #101, NEWBERG, OR 97132

www.barclaypress.com

To
Samuel Milo,
whose grandmother prays he will grow up
to be a man of faith.

CATCHING THEIR TALK IN A BOX

The Life-Story of Joy Ridderhof

GEORGE FOX PRESS
Life-Story
MISSIONS
SERIES

© 1987 George Fox Press

Library of Congress Catalog Card Number: 87-81296

International Standard Book Number: 0-943701-13-9

First printing–1987
Second printing–1990
Third printing–2001
Fourth printing–2002
Fifth printing–2003

Cover by Jannelle Loewen

Printed in the United States of America

CONTENTS

1. Something New to Think About 1
2. A Change of Plans 9
3. A Fifteen-Dollar Beginning 17
4. From Stable To Studio 23
5. Off to the North 31
6. The Hitchhiker 39
7. Many Hold-Uppers! 45
8. The Bright Red Box 53
9. Under the Baobab Tree 61
10. One Large Gift 71

Life-Story
MISSIONS
SERIES

BY BETTY M. HOCKETT

From Here to There and Back Again
the life-story of Dr. Charles DeVol,
missionary to China and Taiwan

What Will Tomorrow Bring?
the life-story of Ralph and Esther Choate,
missionaries to Burundi, Africa

Down a Winding Road
the life-story of Roscoe and Tina Knight,
missionaries to Bolivia, Peru, and Mexico City

Happiness Under the Indian Trees
the life-story of Catherine Cattell,
missionary to India and Taiwan

Catching Their Talk in a Box
the life-story of Joy Ridderhof,
founder of Gospel Recordings

Mud on Their Wheels
the life-story of Vern and Lois Ellis,
missionaries to the Navajo Indians

Whistling Bombs and Bumpy Trains
the life-story of Anna Nixon, missionary to India

Keeping Them All in Stitches
the life-story of Geraldine Custer,
missionary to Burundi, Africa

No Time Out
the life-story of George and Dorothy Thomas, missionaries
to Burundi and Rwanda, Africa, and the Navajo Indians

Outside Doctor on Call
the life-story of Ezra and Frances DeVol,
missionaries to China, India, and Nepal

Chapter 1

SOMETHING NEW TO THINK ABOUT

Regular – r-e-g-u-l-a-r! The milkman goes on his regular *route. Arithmetic – a-r-t-h . . . ! No! That's not right. It's a-r-i-t-h-m-e-t-i-c! I can do three* arithmetic *problems today!*

Eight-year-old Joy Ridderhof stared at the green and yellow flowered wallpaper behind the kitchen table. Her left hand clutched the round, red baking powder can. A tin measuring cup dangled from the other. *I can't go on to the next spelling list 'til I get these words right!* Joy thought impatiently.

"Joy!" her mother scolded. "Not a *cup* of baking powder! A tablespoonful!" Mrs. Ridderhof sighed and jerked the cup out of Joy's hand. "You're more trouble than you're worth in the kitchen. If you could only keep your mind on things! Go on and get ready for church. I'll mix these pancakes up myself!"

"Yes, Mother," replied Joy. She sauntered through the dining room and parlor, then upstairs to her attic bedroom in the big cream-colored house on the hill. *Governor – g-o-v-r-n . . . ! Oh dear, I always leave out the e. Why do we have to have such hard words!*

Joy found the blue-and-white Sunday dress and slipped it over her head. She poked one foot into a brown shoe, then stood, holding the other. More spelling words popped up like jack-in-the-boxes.

Suddenly, she heard, "Joy!" and older sister Amy rushed in. "Don't you know the rest of us are at the table waiting breakfast for you?"

Amy frowned. "I 'spose you were daydreaming again. You're so absentminded, Joy! Here, let me quick tie your sash. There's not time to braid your hair new. Just brush it up some and tie the blue ribbon around."

Joy pushed the spelling words aside. She could worry more about them later.

"I won't tease you this time," David promised as Joy slid into her chair. She smiled and shrugged her shoulders. Joy knew she made it fun for David by nearly always falling for his pranks.

"Fraidy cat!" whispered Stanley on her left. "You're afraid of most everything – even that teeny-weeny harmless spider you saw on the wall last night!"

Joy glared at this brother before she scooted her chair closer to big sister Rosa and leaned forward to smile at their other sister, Susan.

None of Joy's family there at 122 Witmer Street in Los Angeles, California, could ever have guessed that Joy would turn out to be somebody famous. If anybody had said as much, they would have replied, "Not our day-dreaming little sister!"

The Ridderhof family attended church regularly. There, Joy learned about sin and salvation. One day, at age 13, she accepted Jesus as her Savior. Later she went forward to pray at the altar.

"Now I know for sure I'm saved," she said afterward.

Joy became an enthusiastic Christian. As she grew up, she eagerly took part in the church activities. She especially enjoyed the good times with the young people. Her friends noticed how she did her best to help others know Christ as their Savior, too.

She had always been a smiley person. Her blue eyes twinkled and her round cheeks grew even more round when she smiled. Most people thought of her as a happy young woman.

At times, though, Joy said things that made people hurry the other direction. "Don't bother me! Can't you see I'm studying for the final exam tomorrow? I don't dare fail! And if you people don't leave me alone I think I'll go crazy!"

Or, "I'm so worried about giving this report in front of the class next Tuesday. I don't see how I can ever do it!"

Always, however, Joy was immediately sorry. *I don't like what's happening inside of me*, she thought. *It's wrong. I'm a Christian. I shouldn't worry and be so cross with people. But how can I be different?*

Just before the end of that school term, Dr. R. C. McQuilkin came to preach at her church. Although she didn't know it, that week would end up as one of the most important times in her life.

But this is final exam week, she fretted. *I don't have time to go to evening services.* She worried awhile longer and then finally said, *I'll go this once and study the rest of the week.*

Dr. McQuilkin's first message soon made Joy forget all about her studies.

"Worry is sin," he said emphatically. "If you trust God, you don't worry. If you worry, you don't trust God!"

Joy gasped and sat up straighter. *He's preaching right at me!* she thought.

"We must always rejoice," he went on to say. "We must give thanks to God at all times for all things."

These were new ideas to Joy: Worry is sin ... trust God ... rejoice always!

I want to hear more, she decided. *I'll go to the meetings every night, even though I should study.*

As Dr. McQuilkin preached, God spoke to Joy. "From now on, I want you to trust Me for everything."

A powerful feeling of love for God swept over Joy. More than anything else, she wanted to trust Him and find out what He could do in her life.

4

Yes, Lord, I'll do my best to have complete faith in You, she promised. *And I'll praise You because You can bring good out of everything.* Then she added firmly, *And I'll rejoice – always!*

From then on, Joy's life changed.

One day Dr. McQuilkin said, "I plan to start a Bible school in Columbia, South Carolina."

Joy immediately wanted to go there. When she looked at the map, she thought sadly, *South Carolina is too far away. I don't have enough money to get there.* Distance and dollars were obstacles as big as the blue-gray mountains she saw from her bedroom window every day.

"I would so much like to go to your Bible school," Joy told Dr. McQuilkin. "It doesn't seem possible, though."

"The Lord will guide you," he answered simply.

It hadn't occurred to Joy that God guided people in practical things like going to school. She talked to Him about it. *Lord, guide me in the way You want me to go. I want to be sure to fit into Your plan.* And, since she wanted to trust God, she added, *If you want me at Columbia Bible School, You'll have to pay my fare.*

Soon after that, Joy received a letter from her sister Susan who lived in Minneapolis, Minnesota. "If we pay your fare here and back," Susan wrote, "would you come and help me for a few weeks?"

Suddenly she had new hope! *It would cost about the same for me to travel from Minneapolis to South Carolina as it would to come from*

Minneapolis back to Los Angeles, Joy thought. *Susan can pay my bus fare from Minnesota to South Carolina!*

And so it happened. Joy went to Minneapolis to help Susan, and then on to Columbia, South Carolina. She arrived in time for the first classes at the new Bible school.

By this time Joy had decided God wanted her to be a missionary to Ethiopia, Africa. *Being here at Columbia Bible School is the first step to going to Africa,* she thought happily.

Her parents had agreed to pay the $25 monthly school fee. Still, she had one other important question: What about money for clothes and other necessary things?

Before, Joy would have worried herself into a frenzy. Now she said confidently, "God says He will supply all our needs. I will trust Him instead of worrying."

She found out that God did what He promised. The amount of money she needed always came at the right time. *God is never late!* she thought, being careful to thank Him.

"It's important to thank God for all the happy things He does for me in answer to my prayers," she explained to a friend.

It seemed easy to rejoice for so many good things at Columbia Bible School. There were times yet to come, though, when most people wouldn't find much to rejoice about.

*   *   *

Joy finished as one of the first three graduates of Columbia Bible School. After that she worked in a church in Florida for a year. Then she returned to the big cream-colored house at 122 Witmer Street.

"Now I'll get ready to go to Ethiopia as a missionary," she said.

When she asked about it, this reply came back: "There is not enough money to send new missionaries now."

Someone offered to pay her way. Still there were no opportunities to go to Ethiopia. "I suppose I'll have to wait and go to Africa next year," she said.

"Wait another year?" asked a surprised friend. "But Joy, if you wait that long, some people will miss out on hearing the Gospel!"

"Oh, my!" Joy exclaimed. "But there's not any way for me to go to Africa now."

Not long after that God said to Joy, "There are people in other places of the world besides Africa. They need to hear about Me, too."

This was something else new to think about!

I've always considered Africa as the mission field, she thought. *Now I believe God is saying the whole world is a mission field.*

Suddenly she dropped to her knees beside her bed. "Lord!" she cried, "Anywhere You want me to go, I'll go!"

After praying, Joy was certain that anywhere still meant somewhere in Africa.

Joy and her little brother.

Joy leaving on her first missionary assignment to Honduras.

8

Chapter 2

A CHANGE OF PLANS

The next Sunday a member of the California Friends mission board asked Joy, "Would you be willing to go to Honduras as a missionary? There's a great need there."

"Honduras?" she replied. "That's in Central America. The idea of going there doesn't appeal to me at all! Besides, God wants me to go to Africa. I'd really rather go there!"

That afternoon Joy casually pulled out a Scripture card from a small box called a Promise Box. She read these words: "The Lord shall command the blessing upon thee...in all that thou settest thine hand unto; and he shall bless thee in the land which the Lord thy God giveth thee. Deuteronomy 28:8"

Joy knew God was speaking to her again. "He wants me to go to Honduras. There's no doubt about it!" she said.

*   *   *

9

In a few months, Joy arrived in Tegucigalpa, the crowded capital city of Honduras. *The streets are so narrow and gloomy*, she thought with disappointment. In her mind, mission work meant being out in the jungle. Or at least in a small village.

Before long, though, excitement replaced her first dismal impressions. Joy loved the people, and wished she could talk to them in their own Spanish language.

She began to study Spanish. *This is as difficult as learning spelling words used to be*, she thought.

After lots of hard work she knew many Spanish words and how to put them together to make sentences. People sometimes laughed at her comical mistakes. "Oh! That's the wrong word?" Joy would ask, then laugh, and bravely try to say it correctly.

Even while she studied Spanish, Joy energetically helped with the mission work. She enjoyed the open-air meetings as well as visiting sick people in the hospital. When people came to the altar at the chapel meetings, she gladly prayed with them.

Mrs. Dorothy Cammack, the missionary in charge, often took Joy along when she traveled to country villages. These trips usually began with the two of them riding on buses bulging with people and freight. Later they transferred to mules, bumping along skinny trails that crisscrossed the mountainsides. On one of these trips they stopped at a town called Marcala.

"A missionary used to live here," Dorothy explained. "Now the only believers are a little group of poor, uneducated women. They don't have a leader."

These Christian women welcomed the visitors enthusiastically. Joy and Dorothy encouraged the believers to keep on obeying God. They all prayed together.

When the time came for Joy and Dorothy to leave, the village women asked, "Will you come back again soon?"

I wish we could, Joy thought. *They don't have anyone to teach them. I'm sorry we have to leave already.*

The missionaries climbed back on their mules and bounced along to another village. Joy couldn't forget the little group of faithful women in Marcala.

On their way back to Tegucigalpa, Joy and Dorothy stopped in Marcala again. Joy was sorry when they had to leave this time, too. *I feel as if I belong here*, she thought.

She still felt that way when they got back to the capital city. Joy asked God what He wanted her to do, and in a few days she told the other missionaries, "God is calling me to work in Marcala."

"But it wouldn't be safe for you to live alone out there," Dorothy insisted.

"God will take care of me," Joy answered courageously.

Finally Dorothy said, "There is a mission house there, and those few believers. But, you can't go alone. You must have someone with you who knows the customs of the country and who will protect you and help you with the marketing and housework."

"I will go with you," volunteered Cruzita, a sturdy young Honduran woman.

Joy smiled and clasped Cruzita's hands in hers. "God always knows just what I need!" she answered. This Christian friend proved willing for any kind of work, a good helper for Joy.

Since there were only a few foreigners in Marcala, everyone noticed Joy. Curious villagers gathered around when she appeared on the streets each Sunday for an open-air meeting. Even the men hurried away from their drinking to have a look at the white señorita.

God soon showed what He could do.

Juan, the son of Joy's cook, became sick. "He will die!" his mother cried.

"We must pray!" Joy said. "We'll rejoice because we'll be able to see how God works. You know, He can heal Juan's body and also save his soul."

They prayed and God answered! Soon Juan was healed. Joy and her friends rejoiced all the more.

God took care of Joy when villagers objected to her street meetings. He also protected her and other believers as angry people threatened them because they believed in God. He kept Joy safe during intense fighting among the Hondurans.

At the time of one revolution, twenty people stayed with Joy at the mission house. They didn't dare go out to buy food.

One day Joy announced, "There's no food left. Now's the time to rejoice because we know God has promised to take care of us. He will hear us when we pray."

After they finished praying, Joy said, "The answer must be on the way. Let's expect it."

She went to the door and looked up and down the dirty village street. *How will God answer our prayer?* she wondered.

And then she saw something. "There's Juan leading a pack mule this way!" she shouted. "Maybe he has something for us!" They waited excitedly.

Juan arrived at Joy's doorstep in a few minutes. He explained that his mule-load of supplies had been sent by missionaries in another place.

"How wonderful!" Joy exclaimed. "I'm so glad we trusted God!" She smiled a smile that looked as if it would never go away. Then she added, "Now we must thank Him, and we'll thank the missionaries, too. Never forget—God is always on time!"

Joy often invited children and needy adults to stay with her so she could take care of them. Her own money dwindled but she rejoiced anyway. "It'll be exciting to see how God provides this time," she would say.

She didn't have time to think about getting new clothes when the old ones wore out. But somehow, packages with dresses and shoes inside arrived from the United States at the right times.

"Just what I need!" Joy said happily. "How did they know? And look, everything fits perfectly! Thank You, Lord Jesus!"

Later, when telling how it happened, she said, "God *never* failed."

Joy worked hard. Her days began at four o'clock in the morning—the time she and the girls who lived in her home had prayer and Bible studies together. Another group of people came for Bible study at 5:30. Others came for more studies an hour later. Many of the people in Marcala accepted Jesus as their Savior. Joy continually praised God for answers to prayer.

Thirteen villages were located close to Marcala. "They're also my responsibility," Joy said. She spent lots of time traveling along muddy trails or across flooding rivers to visit the people there.

Many of the villagers could not read or write. *But they need to know what the Bible says,* Joy thought. *The only way is for them to memorize the verses.*

She organized a plan for helping these people learn a Bible verse. Joy slowly said one phrase. They repeated it back to her. They learned the next phrase the same way. Over and over she helped them say the words. Later she went back to make sure they could still say the verse.

This slow, painstaking method made good preparation for work Joy would do a few years later.

She also ministered to people when they were sick with flu or more serious illnesses, such as smallpox and malaria. Daily living in the village took Joy's energy. Still she kept on, not complaining. It didn't matter that she often went without things she needed in order to help others. Instead, she rejoiced.

Many Hondurans accepted Jesus. This made Joy so happy she scarcely noticed the nervous twitch on the left side of her face. Or that she had lost weight because of not eating properly.

One day another missionary came for a visit. Joy's appearance startled her. "Joy! You're sick! You need to go somewhere for a complete rest and to see a doctor. I think something serious is happening to you! It could affect your health for the rest of your life."

"I guess I haven't been feeling too well," Joy admitted quietly. "I've wondered why I get so tired. It's been six years since I came. Maybe it's time for me to take a vacation. But I hate to leave. The people need me!"

Even so, Joy got ready to go back to the United States as soon as she could. "I'm going quickly," she told her village friends, "so I can come back sooner!"

As it happened, it was eight years before Joy returned to Honduras.

Hand cranked phonographs ready for shipment to Peruvian jungles and the simple "Card Talk" phonograph. The record is turned by a pencil or stick.

Chapter 3

A FIFTEEN-DOLLAR BEGINNING

Joy went home to the cream-colored house at 122 Witmer Street. "A few weeks of rest and I'll be able to get back to the work," she told her family and friends.

The illness, however, didn't go away. Praying and rejoicing didn't seem to make any difference.

God spoke to Joy during those discouraging days. "All of this will turn out for your good," He said. "I have a wonderful purpose for your life, even though you do not understand it now."

"Thank You, Lord!" Joy replied. "I do want to trust You!" By then it was past the return-to-Marcala date, but Joy found comfort in God's promises. Isaiah 43:15 was a favorite: "Behold I will do a new thing...."

She also discovered Revelation 3:8: "Behold, I have set before thee an open door, and no man can shut it." Joy read it many times, and then thought, *There's always something on the other side of an open door. I believe God is telling me*

17

He has other things for me to do while I wait to go back to Honduras. Sickness or no sickness, God is going to do something special for me.

Joy didn't forget her friends in Honduras. She thought about the little huts clumped together in tiny villages or scattered over the mountains. The people were interested in the Gospel when they had the opportunity to hear it. *But how will they hear?* she wondered. *I can't go back yet, and most of the people can't read!*

She remembered a poor and sad and worried widow with many children. *She couldn't memorize even one verse!* Joy recalled. *I tried all day to help her but she was too weak with hunger. When will she ever hear someone repeating Scripture in her own language again?*

All at once Joy perked up. *I know a man in Honduras who has a phonograph in his store. If only that poor little widow could have a Spanish gospel record to play on it! She could hear the Scripture again and again. And others could, too.*

But the man with the phonograph had already told Joy, "I have no Christian records!" Furthermore, when Joy looked, she couldn't find Spanish Scripture records or songs anywhere.

Joy began to daydream. *A gospel record in Spanish... Oh, I wish... But I can't do anything about making one....*

Gradually, however, she decided, *There is something I can do about it! We'll have to make Spanish Gospel records!*

From that day on, God began to turn this new thing He had promised into something greater than she had ever dreamed of.

Joy made definite plans. "We'll need music, so I must learn to play the guitar," she said. While she recuperated, she took guitar lessons.

Although she felt better, Joy still didn't have much strength. She didn't have any money or experience in making records, either. But, as she prayed about it, she knew God wanted her to continue. "God will supply all I need," she said, and started to plan the program for the first record.

There'll be music that the Honduran people like. Also Bible verses and comments – all in the Spanish language, she noted.

God helped Joy meet a Christian man who had excellent recording equipment. "Yes, I'll be glad to help you," he said.

They completed the first master record on December 31, 1938. It cost $15. She paid for it with money her friends had given.

Joy eagerly listened to the record. As the songs and Bible verses came through clearly, her excitement grew. "I'm sure the people will love it!" she said, smiling contentedly.

She ordered 24 copies, and right away shipped them off to Honduras. The records quickly became a success. Christians listened to them eagerly. Unbelievers did, too.

"I'll go back to Marcala when I've produced 50 record programs," she announced.

Before Joy knew it, she was working as ambitiously as she had in Marcala. She wrote letters, organized programs for more records, and packed the records for shipping. Her tiny attic bedroom at 122 Witmer Street was aclutter with this new activity.

Joy paid the technician after each recording session. Sometimes it cost $16, sometimes $32, depending on the amount of time she used the studio. As people contributed money, she put it in a dresser drawer in her room. One evening before going to the studio, she counted the coins and bills.

"Oh dear," she said. "There's not even half enough to pay what I'll owe tonight."

God reminded her, "Joy, you promised to trust Me for everything."

"Yes, Lord, I know!" she answered. "Well, we'll go on tonight as planned. It's too late to cancel, anyway." She felt sure God would not fail, although she couldn't imagine what He would do.

The recording went well. Afterward, Joy walked slowly to the desk, looking at her little dab of money. She wondered what to say. The technician sat busily adding and subtracting numbers on the paper before him.

Joy waited quietly.

Soon the young man looked up. "Miss Ridderhof, I've been going over your account and I see I've made a mistake. I owe you money!" He told her the amount. It was exactly enough to finish paying for that evening's work.

"Thank You, Lord," Joy whispered. That night she smiled more than usual.

*　　*　　*

Joy hadn't thought about making records in other languages. Spanish-speaking people around the world, though, were already listening to the first records.

Then one day she received a letter from a missionary, asking, "Would you consider producing records in the Navajo Indian language if we pay for them? The Navajos worship many gods, not just the one, true God. Many of them don't read. Those who live way out on the reservation are far from churches. Most of the missionaries do not speak the Navajo language, even if they could get around to see all of the Indians."

The idea attracted Joy. *The Navajos must have records in their language, too*, she thought. *And I believe God wants me to take on this additional project. I just don't want anything to hinder me from going back to Honduras.*

Blessing and courage refreshed Joy like a cool breeze on a hot day. *Lord, I'll make recordings in as many languages as You want me to*, she promised.

That decision would soon lead Joy into places she had never once dreamed of going.

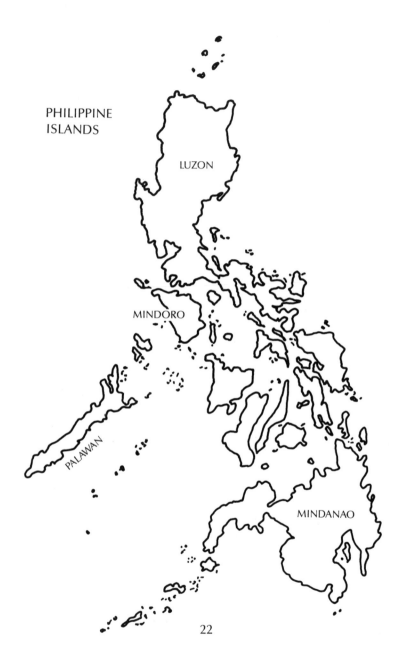

PHILIPPINE
ISLANDS

LUZON

MINDORO

PALAWAN

MINDANAO

22

Chapter 4

FROM STABLE TO STUDIO

"It takes an amazing amount of time to produce one record," Joy told a friend.

She wrote scripts and located people to speak and sing who were native to the languages she recorded. "That way the listeners won't think the Gospel is just a white man's religion," she explained. She also wrote letters to missionaries, letting them know they could order the records.

Envelopes, stamps, carbon paper, hymnbooks, and stacks of music filled Joy's attic room. Ann Sherwood, Joy's friend, said one day, "What if I came two afternoons a week to help?"

"I could use your help, all right!" Joy answered with a wide smile. But I couldn't pay you."

"Where do you get your money?" Ann asked.

"I just tell the Lord what I need. This is God's work so I trust Him to provide. And you know, Ann, He always does!"

"I can trust Him, too," Ann replied.

Joy and Ann had no idea their conversation was the start of an organization that would reach around the world. At first they called it "Spanish Gospel Recordings." Soon, however, they shortened the name to "Gospel Recordings."

Before long Joy told Ann, "We must have a recording studio of our own. We'll ask God to provide it for us. In the meantime we'll rejoice even though it's frustrating to plan studio time around other people's schedules."

One day Joy noticed the tumbledown building in the backyard next door. It had been there as long as she could remember. At first it had housed horses. For a long time there hadn't been anything in it except junk.

All at once she imagined the old stable as something entirely different.

Joy rushed out to investigate. The dirt floor spread out unevenly between crooked walls. Broken doors hung at lopsided angles.

"But the roof's good," she said. "I believe God directed my attention to this old shed. If we clean it up and repair it, it'll be a good place for our recording studio."

Joy and Ann prayed about it. After some time, the Lord made it possible for them to buy that property. Then, while Joy and a few others scrubbed and painted the old stable, the carpenters hammered and sawed. Electricians volunteered their work, too. Someone else donated good furniture while others gave money to pay for the building materials. A generous friend sent over a piano and another provided used recording equipment.

The old stable turned into a usable sound-proof studio, with space left over for a secretary.

God also provided the secretary. Her name was Virginia Miller. She became the third member of the staff.

Joy and Ann quickly learned how to use their new equipment, and were soon making records in several languages.

*　　*　　*

Shortly after this, World War II began, causing shortages in supplies for making records. One morning they had only one acetate record blank left for cutting records.

"That's not even enough for our work today," Joy observed.

"For once we have plenty of money on hand but no supplies to spend it on," Ann said.

"We must pray," Joy said, kneeling by a chair. Virginia and Ann knelt, also.

They had just started praying when they heard a knock at the front door. They ignored it and kept praying. Insistent knocks interrupted them again, this time at the back door. Ann tiptoed to see who was there.

She opened the door and a delivery woman said curtly, "I've brought 300 acetate record blanks from the warehouse. Here, take 'em!"

"Joy! Come quickly!" Ann hollered. "God has already answered our prayers."

Wartime restrictions also made it nearly impossible for people from other nations to come to Los Angeles to make recordings. "We'll just have to go to them," Joy announced. "And now we do have a recording machine we can use away from the studio."

The women had already received an invitation to make recordings in Mexico. Joy thought, *That will be our first work trip away from Witmer Street.*

They flew into a flurry of preparations. "We'll need a vehicle," they said. "A station wagon would be good for hauling our recording equipment." Gas was rationed during wartime, so they also needed extra coupons to buy gas for the trip.

Three days before time to go, they still didn't have a car. "God will provide," Joy said with faith. "He's always on time."

She felt confident as she went to the special office to ask for the extra gas ration coupons.

"I don't think a trip like this is necessary in war-time," the man behind the counter said. "I can't give you coupons for such a trip. In fact, Miss Ridderhof, your organization is already receiving more gas coupons than necessary. We'll have to cut down on the number we give you."

Now there wouldn't even be enough gas for their work at home—certainly not enough for trips anywhere else. Joy slowly left the office. This time she couldn't say, "Let's rejoice!"

Did I make a mistake? she wondered as she trudged dejectedly up the stairs to her little room. She sighed and knelt down to pray.

Just then, Ann burst into the room without knocking. "Joy, sit down! I have something to tell you," she said solemnly.

What now? thought Joy. *Is she sick, and we can't go?* She lay back on her bed.

Then Ann shouted, "We've got a car! It's loaned to us for as long as we need it!"

Before Joy had time to think what Ann had just said, the rest of the explanation tumbled out. "I went to my doctor for a physical exam to make sure I was okay for the trip to Mexico. Afterward he asked how we were getting there. I said we planned to drive but we didn't have a car yet."

Ann rushed her words together so fast, Joy could hardly keep up.

"Then the doctor said he knew where he could get one for us if it wasn't already sold!"

Joy's smile stretched wider and wider as Ann continued. "He quickly made a phone call and found out this Pontiac station wagon was still for sale. So, he bought it! It's ours to use!"

"Praise the Lord! How wonderful!" Joy exclaimed.

Then her smile disappeared. "But the official refused my request and we can't get the gas!" Her voice had suddenly gone flat.

"Oh, I forgot to say that gas coupons come with the car," Ann answered cheerily. "The man who owned the Pontiac had planned to drive it to Mexico so he had the extra coupons. He sold the car because he decided to go by plane instead. So, see, we have everything we need!"

*　　*　　*

Soon after Joy and Ann arrived in Mexico, God directed them to a certain man. "You may set up your equipment in my new recording studio," he said. "I'm not ready to use it yet!"

During the ten months they worked in Mexico they recorded 400 master records in 33 tribal languages. At the end of that time, they were tired but pleased. And, before they went back home, they couldn't resist doing a little work in Guatemala, too.

"Our first recording trip away from Los Angeles has been successful, thanks to God's help," Joy reported. "We're trusting the Lord to use these messages to help many people."

They returned to Los Angeles by way of Marcala, Honduras. Joy felt like she had been gone only eight days, not eight years. Many people welcomed her with smiles and hugs. For two wonderful weeks Joy and her friends talked and prayed and sang together.

"I can't stay any longer," she explained when it was time to leave. "God has given me another job to do so that many other people will hear about Him." She told how she and her helpers were making records.

The people she loved so much and who also loved her understood. "Yes, you must get on with the work God asked you to do. You will be our missionary. We will pray for you, and we will have a part in what you are doing," they said.

This unexpected blessing gave Joy extra reason to praise the Lord as they returned home to Los Angeles.

* * *

Joy, Ann, and Virginia began to pray about other workers to join them. More and more work was coming to Gospel Recordings and the women needed additional help. They especially needed someone to deal with the mechanical problems.

God soon answered prayer. Several men and women joined the staff at just the time each one was most needed.

That year Joy went on a speaking tour into Washington state. She also attended a prayer conference there. The leader said, "God wants us to give thanks to Him and tell Him our needs. The Bible says we are to 'pray without ceasing.'"

"Yes, I know the importance of prayer," Joy thought. That day she decided again that prayer must continue as the most important part of Gospel Recordings.

The next time she called her workers on Witmer Street, she asked, "How are things going?"

"We're terribly busy," they replied. "We can't get it all done on time."

"Then take a whole day off every week for prayer," Joy said. "God can *work* while we *pray*!"

The staff did as she wanted, although at first some of them grumbled, "We'll never get through all this work if we take a whole day off to pray."

In a few weeks they discovered they were doing more work than ever before. Things happened they never thought possible. After that, the entire staff reserved every Wednesday as the special day of prayer.

Joy realized there were some people who were too poor to pay even a few cents for a record. What if they never heard the Good News that Jesus came to save them and that their sins could be forgiven? She couldn't bear to think that anyone might be left out.

"We won't charge for the records anymore," she said. "We'll give them away free to all who need them. The Gospel is free and so should our records be. We'll trust God to supply the money to make them."

The Gospel Recordings staff soon had special reasons to praise God. They had produced and sent out almost twice as many records as at any other time. "God always provides what we need at exactly the right time," Joy said gratefully.

No one knew then that the next few years would bring even more miracles!

Chapter 5

OFF TO THE NORTH

"The Lord has made it clear He wants us to drive to Alaska and do recording there," Joy and Ann said as they discussed their plan with the staff once more.

"Just you two alone? Clear up there?" some of the workers asked with concern.

"God will go with us!" Joy explained in her usual confident manner. "So many of the Eskimos and Indians live in isolated places. In the winter the snow and ice completely cut them off from missionaries. Records are almost the only way they can hear the Gospel in their own languages."

Upon hearing of the trip, well-meaning friends made dire predictions: "The highway is impossible, and it isn't finished yet...a trip like that is too dangerous for women...you'll perish on the way!"

Since Joy was sure God wanted them to take this trip, she and Ann made plans. "We need a lightweight recording machine," said Joy.

Ann agreed. "We can't possibly transport this heavy equipment in a canoe or small plane.

Remember the new tape recorder we read about? That's exactly what we need!"

Joy nodded and smiled. "But since we don't have enough money, we'd better not order it."

Joy and Ann left Los Angeles on June 7, 1947, headed to the far north, 4,500 miles away. They drove the dark blue 1947 Pontiac someone had loaned to them for this trip.

That night God spoke to Joy about ordering the lightweight tape recorder. "We do need it," she told Ann. "We won't be able to accomplish all we hope to in Alaska if we don't have it. God has promised to supply our needs, so I believe He'll help us have money to pay for the recorder. We won't tell anyone we need money. We'll simply trust God."

Joy telephoned a friend who earlier had offered to sell the equipment to them at a reduced price. "Please deliver the package to us when we're in Montana," she said, giving the proper address.

The two women stopped at several places for speaking engagements, but they didn't mention needing money. In every meeting, people were interested in hearing about the records. "We want you to have this money to help with your work," many said.

By the time Joy and Ann arrived at the Montana address, they had enough money to pay for the new tape recorder! They even had a few cents left over.

Joy and Ann arrived safely in Fairbanks at the home of their friends who had encouraged them to come.

"Thank the Lord," they wrote back to the staff in Los Angeles. "God is so good to us! No car trouble of any kind. We had our first flat tire as we stopped here in front of the house! Before us lies Alaska. Our task is impossible, but you will pray and God will do wonders."

The two women stayed a few days to rest and plan. Then they drove through the dazzling sunlight to the Copper River Indian Valley, far into Alaska. "Look at those beautifully bright wildflowers," Joy exclaimed. "It's hard to imagine that in a few months this landscape will be pure white with deep snow and freezing temperatures."

"That means we must hurry and get started with our work," Ann said.

Soon they met the young missionary man and his wife who would be their helpers. "We'll need to plan our time carefully," Ann reminded. "There's so much to do in such a short time."

They talked about the Kotzebue, Kuskokwim, Diomede, and Malemute dialects they wanted to record.

"This reminds me of the tribes in the Philippine Islands," said the missionary man. "There are a lot of different languages there, too. I was a soldier in the islands during the war. Most of the tribes living back in the mountains don't have any of the Gospel in their own dialects."

Joy would not be able to forget what the young man had just said.

That night she and Ann settled into their sleeping bags in the front and back seats of the Pontiac. Joy's thoughts began to ramble. She pictured the huge complex of over 7,000 islands located between the China Sea and the Pacific Ocean.

But Lord, she prayed, *we've just started on this trip. Are you wanting me to already think about going to the Philippine Islands?*

Soon, Joy and Ann set out on their recording trips, traveling over a vast amount of Alaska. They went by car, train, bus, fishing boats, motorboats, and in an Eskimo skin boat. They flew in both big and little planes.

Missionaries and other Christians received them hospitably everyplace they went. Their hosts always offered the best overnight facilities they had. Sometimes Joy and Ann slept in good beds, but most often they stayed all night in their car, in trailers, in boats, and once in a hayloft. A few times they found themselves sleeping on floors or on church benches.

The women enjoyed food they had never tasted before— caribou and reindeer steaks, savory moose roast, and bear meat that Joy described as "not half bad." They were enchanted at the sight of moose, bears, foxes, whales, sea lions, porpoises, and caribou.

Several times Joy and Ann almost gave up trying to record more languages. The weather often appeared impossible, and difficulties in arranging transportation added to the problems. Every time, however, God worked miracles, making it possible for them to travel to one more place to record one more language.

One trip for one language went this way: fourteen hours on the train; one and a half hours by airplane; four hours on a mail boat; overnight on a large steamer; five hours on a fishing boat.

After they returned to Fairbanks, Joy wrote to the folks at Witmer Street, "We had a wonderful time on that distant island, making records and translating songs into their unwritten language. We were blessed to find Christians who agreed to work with us. They faithfully interpreted the messages in their own language, speaking them into the microphone."

Joy and Ann became fond of the Siberian Eskimos. These brown-skinned people lived in tiny, lonely-looking villages along the lakes, bays, inlets, and rivers. Their sod-and-log igloos formed perfect reflections in the shiny blue water.

The two women did their recording inside the Eskimo igloos. Children and their happy chatter made pleasant background sounds.

Sometimes the recording team worked with people who could not read. At those times Joy began by reciting one phrase. Their Eskimo helper interpreted it into his language.

Together they practiced the words over and over. Finally Ann turned on the tape recorder and the helper said the phrase once more. After that, they went on to the next phrase and did it all again. This arduous process continued for each record.

"Oh, how I thank God you have come," one young woman told them. "I have prayed and cried because of the ache in my heart for my people. They live on an island over 2,000 miles from here. They have no gospel witness at all. I long for them to hear about God and be saved. Now they can hear in our own language on the records. My prayers are answered and I am so happy!"

Another Indian woman said, "I believe God sent you all the way from California just for me!"

Afterwards, as Joy thought about all of the miracles God performed for her and Ann in Alaska, she said, "I wonder why God went to so much trouble for the people in Alaska?"

Someone quickly answered, "Because He loves them so much."

This trip to the far north was strength-taking. But even so, Joy kept thinking about the Philippine Islands. When they arrived back in Los Angeles after five months, she knew where they would go on their next trip.

* * *

"It will take you a hundred years to do all you want to do there," a man told them.

"Recording languages in the Philippine Islands will be God's work," Joy reminded him. "He has never failed us yet, and I'm expecting Him to supply all we need just as He's done before."

One of their first needs was money to pay for passports. They couldn't leave the country without them. *We each need nine dollars*, thought Joy, knowing they didn't have even that small amount. "And this is the day to get the passports."

"Thank You, Lord," said Joy that afternoon, after they had received enough money to pay for their passports.

Two months later, they needed money to pay for visas, also necessary for traveling out of the country. God made sure they had that money on the right day, too.

While on a trip to Seattle, Washington, Joy received a letter from Virginia Miller. The letter said, "A friend has told us she wants to pay the ticket costs for both you and Ann for your trip to the Philippines."

"Praise the Lord!" said Joy. "God is always so faithful to keep His promises. It's good to trust Him completely."

At last the time came to board the ship for the long trip to Manila. *It does seem strange there are only two of us for this big job*, Joy thought. *It'll be difficult to make recordings among the island tribes.*

Even though she could not possibly know all that lay ahead, she didn't feel overwhelmed. She felt comfortable knowing that God had promised to go with them.

After a few weeks at sea, the ship idled into the harbor at Manila. "What shall we do first?" Joy and Ann asked each other. And then they wondered, *Where should they go? Where would they stay? Who would help them find their way around?*

"I don't suppose anyone will meet us!" Joy said. "I didn't make arrangements like that before we left. And something else just occurred to me, Ann. We may have to pay taxes on all of this recording equipment before we can take it away from the dock. That could amount to a large sum of money."

The ship edged into docking position. *Now what?* Joy wondered.

Eskimos hear the message of Jesus Christ through the records.

Chapter 6

THE HITCHHIKER

Joy and Ann looked intently at the crowd along the dock. One man was waving his hat back and forth high over his head.

"Bob Bowman!" both women shouted.

"That's Bob Bowman from the Far East Broadcasting Company here in Manila!" said Joy excitedly.

"It looks like he's waving at us," Ann remarked. "But how does he know we're on this ship?"

They rushed ashore and joyously greeted Mr. Bowman.

"Just this morning I received word from your office that you were on this ship," he told them. He helped the two collect their great stack of luggage and then he spoke to the officials on the dock.

Joy rejoiced when she saw the dock worker write a big "O.K." on every box and suitcase.

"That means we don't have to pay taxes on them," she told Ann, before thanking God again for His goodness.

Joy and Ann remarked about the bustling crowds and the fast-paced traffic. "We couldn't have managed alone," they agreed. "Aren't we glad God sent such competent help!"

*   *   *

The two of them studied the map of the Philippine Islands. They found out many of the islands were nameless and uninhabited. There were, though, several large islands. Mindanao, to the south, was one of them.

"We could go there to record first," said Joy. "Missionaries would welcome us and provide our transportation."

Next they looked at the map of Palawan, a narrow island. Missionaries lived there, too, but in an almost inaccessible area.

Ann wondered if they should begin their work on Mindoro, another of the large islands. "It's fairly close here," she pointed out. "Although there aren't any missionaries there."

"Or, we could stay here on the island of Luzon," Joy suggested. "We could go up into the Mountain Province. See, Lubuagan is right there in the center." They had already heard about Lubuagan and the dangerous drive up the Chico River Canyon to get there. They also knew about the guerrilla fighters who terrorized the area.

Dr. Otley Beyer, a scientist at the University, tossed in another idea. "Most of the year the roads are impassable here on Luzon," he told her. "There are many landslides when it rains so much."

"When will the dry season come?" Joy inquired.

"Right now," Dr. Beyer replied. "You really should go to the north mountains on Luzon now. Otherwise you won't be able to get there until next year."

"I believe that must be what God wants," Joy said quickly. "But what about a car? Well, if we really need it, God will see that we have it."

After that she went back to more prayer and Bible reading. God showed her the promise in I Chronicles 28:20. "Be strong and of good courage, and do it: Fear not, nor be dismayed: For the Lord God, even my God will be with thee; he will not fail thee nor forsake thee . . . ."

Soon afterward, a missionary friend named Russell Honeywell said, "Joy, the Lord wants me to loan my car to you. It's an old one, though."

"But don't you need it yourself?" Joy asked.

"A friend of mine will let me use his."

"Are you sure?" Ann questioned.

"Yes! See, it's all settled."

"Well, thank you, very much indeed, Russell. This is another one of God's amazing miracles!" Joy said, as she smiled on and on. "No matter that the car's old. God will help it run like a new one."

*　　*　　*

In a few days, Joy and Ann were ready to go to Baguio. They planned to make their first record there. As they drove into the city after dark, Joy praised the Lord. "Thank You for a safe journey."

"In spite of the advice we had about not traveling at night where the terrorists are," Ann added.

They were safe, but they had no idea where to go. And they couldn't see anyone to ask. "We'd better pray before we go on," Joy suggested.

In less than 30 minutes, they were in the home of a friend Joy had first known at Columbia Bible School.

"We prayed, Martha," Joy said to her friend, "and before we knew it God brought along someone who knew that Americans lived nearby. When we got to their home, we found they knew you!" Joy and Martha hugged each other, rejoicing in God's miracle ways.

From there, Joy and Ann began the recording process. Right away they had serious problems. Joy kept track of it all in her diary:

The equipment is not working properly. First one thing and then another goes wrong.

It's too noisy here. Workers are building a chapel nearby. Besides that, there's a dog who barks all the time.

Today I'm sick with a bad cold.

The people here need Jesus so much. They cannot read, and they do not understand much English.

Ann did her best to encourage Joy. "We must rejoice! Remember, God is working even though we are having troubles."

At the end of 11 days, they had finished one record! Eight days later, they drove back to Manila

where they found technicians to repair the equipment. In three days the ladies went back to
Baguio. The day after that they made ten records!

As they traveled in the northern area of Luzon,
Joy and Ann heard many cautions. "It's dangerous
to travel alone, especially at night," people said.

The day they left Bangued, bound for Vigan
and Laoag, they had several delays. "We can't get
there before dark," Joy said.

Just outside of Vigan, they came to a young soldier standing beside the road.

"He wants a ride with us!" said Joy.

"Don't stop!" Ann reminded. "There are too
many bandits. We shouldn't pick anyone up."

"It looks as if he's determined to come anyway,"
Joy answered.

As the car moved past, the soldier jumped and
landed on the running board. He hooked his left
arm over the open window.

The women gasped!

They couldn't go on with the soldier in such a
precarious position.

"It's too dangerous for you to ride like that," Joy
called out. "Sit here beside us."

The hitchhiker opened the door and crowded
into the seat.

After a bit Joy and Ann relaxed. Their pas-
senger seemed well-behaved, although they had a
hard time talking to him.

At last they came to Laoag. "Can you help us
find where we intend to go?" Joy asked the soldier.

He knew exactly how to direct them. The house they needed to find happened to be across the street from his army camp.

"Thank You, God," said Joy. "You gave us protection by using a young man, himself afraid to be alone on the road at night—so afraid he forcefully took a ride with American women he had never seen before."

*   *   *

Joy and Ann met with more delays before they left Laoag, at five o'clock one evening.

"We should get to Banua in three hours," Joy calculated. "We'll stay all night there and go on to Aparri tomorrow."

The bumpy, rutty road twisted through the jungle, first one way, then another. Tall green trees and short green trees huddled together with broad-leafed vines woven throughout. As Joy and Ann bounced on further into the jungle, everything changed from bright to dim.

And then it was dark! "God is with us," the women reminded themselves. But in the next instant they wondered, *Is this a road at all?*

And then the track disappeared entirely! Ann whammed her foot against the brake. The car jerked to a stop!

They couldn't see anything but water.

"What shall we do now?" Joy asked. "This is a river!"

Chapter 7

MANY HOLD-UPPERS!

Joy and Ann stared into the thick curtain of darkness.

"I don't think we dare drive in," said Ann. "The water could be deep. Anyway, I can't see any road on the other side."

"What'll we do about spending the night here beside the river?" Joy asked.

As they were thinking what to do, a feeble light appeared, off to the right. Joy saw the dark outline of a man watching them. She gulped and then leaned out the window.

"Could you show us the way to go?" she inquired.

Without saying a word, the man rolled up his pant legs and stepped into the water. He pointed the way with his flashlight.

Ann released the brake and gently urged the car into the river. She clung to the steering wheel as the car plowed to the other side.

"Now we'll be in Banua soon," Joy said. "Thank the Lord!"

Farther on, they lost the road again. This time they were in a tangle of bushes.

Ann looked at Joy. "We can't go on!"

Joy looked at Ann. "Now what do we do?"

The first thing they thought of was a Bible verse, Proverbs 3:6: "In all thy ways acknowledge Him, and He shall direct thy paths." After that they prayed: "Dear Lord, we ask Thee to guide us now."

They were immediately alert as they heard a crunch and a bump, bump!

"That sounds like an ox cart!" said Joy.

They turned around, squinting into the darkness. They could barely see the ox cart with a man standing alongside.

"Hello!" shouted Ann.

The man remained like a statue.

"He's afraid of us," Joy whispered. She got out of the car and spoke to him quietly. "Can you help us find our way?"

The man took three steps forward and flashed his light. It shone like silver on yet another stream of water just beyond the bushes.

There was nowhere else to go. Again, Ann slowly maneuvered the car into water. She kept her eyes straight ahead, making sure to follow the skimpy beam of light. Finally the car splashed up onto the other bank. There, the trail led away from the water into the jungle.

"I can tell we're still going in the right direction," said Joy, "but where is Banua?"

"Did we miss it?" Ann asked.

At that moment they saw the huge tree! Broken off and flat on the ground, it completely blocked the road.

"Well, this is for sure the end of our travel tonight," Joy said firmly.

Then they discovered a truck, also stopped there.

"How far is it to Banua?" Joy asked the driver.

"That's it!" he answered, and pointed past the fallen tree to a practically invisible hotel.

The women looked over that way in amazement. "That's Banua? Just one building?"

Settling into their room later, they rejoiced and praised God for His miracles.

The next morning Joy and Ann looked out their window. "What an impressive sight!" said Joy. "That's the China Sea and the Pacific Ocean flowing together. We're at the top edge of Luzon."

They continued on their way to towns called Aparri, Dugo, Talo, Gattaran, Amulung, Iguig, and Tuguegarao. Equipment breakdowns delayed them many times.

Joy and Ann always prayed when something didn't work. One day, prayer didn't even seem to help. Then Joy had an idea. "This recorder has joggled up and down all day as we've traveled. Now, let's turn it over and joggle it some more."

After more prayer and the upside-down joggling, the recorder worked.

*   *   *

Joy still wanted to go to Lubuagan, even though the road was bad.

Some advised against it. "Many hold-uppers!" they said.

"We'll trust God," Joy and Ann replied and turned their car up Route 99, Highway No. 11.

"And up it is!" said Joy, soon after they started up the road, one of the highest in the world.

It was 96 miles around the top of the mountain range. The women traveled for seven hours on the first lap of the journey. They drove the next 40 miles in five and one-half hours.

On one side of the road a steep cliff rose hundreds of feet straight up. There wasn't anything on the other side except the valley far below. Part of the time only 12 inches of space separated the car and the sharp drop-off. Several times the soft dirt threatened to pull the car and its passengers over the edge.

The two rejoiced when they finally saw the town of Lubuagan. Mr. Fisher, a missionary, asked, "How did you know this was the one day in the year when it doesn't rain? If it had rained it would have been impossible for you to get here in this car."

Sometime later the women found that many people back home had prayed for their safety.

*   *   *

During this four-month trip into northern Luzon, the women had lots of reasons to remind God about His promises.

The daytime heat felt stifling. Once they lost the rope and the handle for their hand-started generator. They recorded in all kinds of buildings, sometimes in schools, at other times in churches. They became agile at climbing steep ladders into houses. Some had ordinary wooden floors, but in others the bamboo floors seemed shaky.

Their equipment worked and then it didn't. When Joy became sick, they were tempted to ask, "What good can come out of this?"

Joy in the Philippines.

But Joy would remember aloud, "God hasn't promised to always tell us His purposes in allowing troublesome things to happen. We'll just keep on trusting Him and rejoicing."

She had no way of knowing that at least two new workers would join Gospel Recordings after they read about the problems she and Ann had faced in the Philippines. Or that in years to come their faith and trust would inspire others.

One day, Ann wrote a song they sang again and again:

There's a reason—a glorious reason
For everything the Lord may send your way!
When there's nothing going right,
Walk by faith and not by sight—
There's a reason, so REJOICE the live-long day.

* * *

On their way back to Manila, Joy and Ann unexpectedly met Bonefacio, who had been their chauffeur during their first visit. He offered to drive them back to the city in their borrowed car.

"This car drives like a new one!" he exclaimed.

Thank You, Lord, thought Joy.

The five months on Luzon had been productive in spite of the problems. They had recorded 40 languages and dialects.

* * *

Next, Joy carefully studied the map of Mindoro. She began to think about going there, although no missionaries lived on that island.

She made notes to help her get ready for this trip:

1. We can't take the car to Mindoro.
2. We'll travel by bus and boat.
3. It'll be hard to communicate with the tribal people.
4. We won't go unless it's God's will.

Joy spent several days talking to God and filling her mind with His promises. She felt sure Exodus 23:20 had God's special message to her: "Behold I send an angel before thee, to keep thee in the way and to bring thee into the place which I have prepared."

"The Lord wants us to go to Mindoro. He's promised to guide us," she told Ann. "We must prepare to go now."

While Ann edited tapes to send back to Los Angeles, Joy collected the things they needed. "This will be different from any other trip," she decided. "We can't take heavy baggage, only things we can carry."

She wrote "shoes with leather soles" at the top of the list. "Other kinds melt in the rain," she said. Next she set out to find lightweight clothes, raincoats, bedding they could wrap in thin mats, and medicines.

How to carry their recording equipment remained as the biggest question. "It weighs 150 pounds," Joy said with a sigh.

The answer arrived in the mail later that same day.

There's A Reason

2 Cor. 5:7

Ann Sherwood

There's a rea-son a glo-rious rea-son

For ev-'ry-thing the Lord may send your way When

there's noth-ing go-ing right walk by faith and not by sight;

There's a rea-son So RE-JOICE! the live-long day!

Used by permission.

Chapter 8

THE BRIGHT RED BOX

Joy quickly unwrapped the package that had come from her office on Witmer Street. The bright red box, lightweight, only nine inches across and 20 inches long, looked like a toy.

Joy read the note that came with the box.

"It took a lot of hours, with both of us working hard to make this. Now it will do the work for you, and we hope it will be a big help. Sincerely, Al Rethey and Herman Dyk."

Joy turned the bright red box this way and that.

"It must be a battery-powered tape recorder," Ann said. "Remember, you told Herman that's what we needed!"

"That's it!" Joy exclaimed. "Of course that's what it is. Herman and Al have made it for us. Aren't we glad God sent them to be part of our staff!"

The new recorder worked perfectly. Joy squealed with excitement. "Just think, Ann, every-thing we need for recording is right here in this one little red box. It'll be so easy to carry. See, it tucks under one arm quite handily."

One day, they were ready. Clothes, tapes, batteries, and all else they needed for recording had been packed. Off the women went with their nine pieces of luggage.

At first, the bus driver said, "No room!"

However, the kindly ticket man said, "I think we can make room."

He helped Ann into the baggage seat at the back of the bus. Joy squeezed into a seat in the front, next to a quiet little woman. The ticket man sat beside her.

Before long he asked Joy lots of questions. "Where are you going? What is your name? Where will you stay?"

Joy answered and then asked a question of her own. "Do you know of a hotel?"

The man whispered something to the woman squashed between him and Joy.

The lady turned to her and said softly, "You come our house? We poor." She smiled as she added, "We like you come our house!"

She must be his wife, thought Joy, as tears filled her eyes. Here was God's angel, just as He promised. Of course she and Ann would stay at the angel's house!

That night the ticket man introduced the women to his cousin. "Caridad lives on Mindoro. She go tomorrow. She go with you?"

"Oh yes!" replied Joy enthusiastically. She recognized another person God had sent to take care of the details she had dreaded about this trip.

The next day Caridad assisted the Americans. They boarded the boat bound for the town of Nauhan, on Mindoro. There she introduced them to a delightful Filipino man and his wife. They invited Joy and Ann to stay in their home for the month they were on the island.

One of their bus trips away from Nauhan took them to the little village named Bongabong. "We're here to find the Mangyans," Joy and Ann explained to their hosts, Mr. and Mrs. Sulit and their nine children.

"We seldom see them," the Sulits said. "They're afraid of village people. And they don't come at all now during the rainy season."

Joy and Ann asked God's help. "You can do the impossible, Lord. If it's Your will for us to record the language of these mountain people, please send them to us."

God already had set His answer in motion. Two young Mangyan men were on their way to the village. They carried a load of fragrant orchids to sell.

The young men stopped first at the Sulit home.

Mr. Sulit greeted them gently, being careful not to frighten the tribesmen. He bought several of the fragile lavender orchids. "Would you like to see two women with white skin?" he asked. "They're happy and they're kind."

Joy and Ann waited silently, almost afraid to breathe. Would the young men accept the invitation?

Minutes later, Joy whispered, "They're coming in!"

For the rest of that day, and half of the next, they worked steadily at recording. Mr. Sulit interpreted as they recorded a gospel message in words that sounded strange to others. They made perfect sense, however, to these young mountain men:

"Chief of Sky, He who made sky and earth and all in it, He send already message to all people of world. Message this in bundle of leaves they call 'Bundle of leaves what Chief of Sky say', and it tells how Chief of Sky give Son His, He has only one Son, come to earth receive punishment of sins ours...."

Once again Joy rejoiced because God answered their prayers quickly so another tribe could hear the Gospel.

* * *

Next, the recording team went to Palawan. They met a man named Harry Edwards, who had lived and worked there a long time.

"My boy Bert said many years ago the only way to get the Gospel to the people here would be through records and phonographs," he told the women from Gospel Recordings. "But we didn't have any idea how that could be. I read about your work a few months ago and I felt sure you could help us. We didn't think you'd come yourself, though."

*   *   *

Joy and Ann discussed the last phase of their visit to the Philippine Islands. "The beliefs of the people on Mindanao are different from those in the northern islands," said Joy.

This made it necessary for the two of them to spend many hours writing new scripts. At the same time, missionaries prepared travel plans for them.

God worked in surprising ways. Sometimes He surprised a carmel-colored Filipino!

Sinagda had a hard time believing what he heard when Joy played back the recording of his voice. First he smiled and then broke out into noisy laughter. "I am so happy! This is an answer to my prayers. I did not dream such a thing would ever come. I am the only one who preaches in this dialect. I've prayed that someone else would come to learn it so that when my voice is gone they could still hear the good news."

At other times God surprised Joy and Ann!

One day they met a young woman named Lourdes who had a loud voice. "I work at a gold mine," she said. "I find languages for you!"

"This story seems unlikely," Joy thought. But she didn't want to ignore an opportunity that might help them find the Mansaka language.

"Let's go with her, Ann," she suggested.

They boarded a big truck loaded with workers on their way back to the mines. Lourdes became more excited as they went around the last curve into the mine settlement.

After they got off the truck, Joy and Ann stayed close behind Lourdes. She hurried past the lineup of run-down wooden houses, walked up stone steps winding along the hillside, and opened the door to a luxurious cottage.

"My relative is the cook here," Lourdes announced in her ringing voice. "You can stay."

Joy and Ann thanked God for this gift. Running water, hot baths, soft beds, icy drinks, and delicious food were more than they expected from a trip to the gold mines.

There were, however, other surprises!

Lourdes informed them one evening after supper, "That man carrying dishes speak a language."

"What language?" Joy wanted to know.

"He come from Agusan," Lourdes replied. "He travel down river with crocodiles that bite."

"Ann and I hoped to go to Agusan to get the Manobo language," Joy said, "but now we won't have time."

Lourdes assured them it would not be wise to go there, anyway.

Joy repeated her question. "What language does this man speak?"

This time the young man heard and answered for himself. "I am a Manobo from Agusan."

Joy and Ann nodded to each other. "Of course!" Joy said. "God is always faithful!"

As soon as they finished the Manobo recordings, Joy and Ann talked with the mine workers. They spoke Mansaka, exactly what the women were looking for!

Right away Joy discovered a problem. "There are no Mansaka words for happiness and joy," she said to Ann. "And none for Savior, holy, good, love, friend, prayer, or heaven."

"How can we tell the gospel message without those words?" Ann asked.

"We'll rewrite our script," Joy replied. "We can find words they know and go from there."

God helped them with their search for the right words. When the women left the mine settlement, they had finished one more set of recordings.

*   *   *

By this time, Joy and Ann had been on the Philippine Islands for 14 months. They had seen more of the territory than most missionaries would ever see. Joy reported in a newsletter, "We've made 700 separate recordings in 92 languages and dialects. But this is not our accomplishment. It is God's work!"

Sanna, Joy, and Ann on a recording mission trip. Joy playing records for Africans.

Chapter 9

UNDER THE BAOBAB TREE

Joy still did not tell people when she needed money. If anyone asked how her work was financed, she always replied , "It doesn't matter if the need is ten dollars or a thousand dollars. God sends us the right amount by the right day—in answer to our prayers of faith."

Whenever Joy returned home to Witmer Street, she lived in the same plain little attic room. She helped serve the meals and do the dishes along with everyone else. Although she directed the work of Gospel Recordings, she demanded no special privileges.

Her old car rattled and squeaked. Even so, she enjoyed taking visitors for a drive to see the sights of Los Angeles. Often, though, she got side-tracked by describing the wonderful answers to prayer. Sometimes she drove right past whatever she intended to show her guests.

Joy lived so close to God that now and then her friends had a hard time knowing if she was talking to God or to them. She often prayed aloud while she drove as well as when she rode with others. Joy felt free to talk to God about everything, at any time or place.

She had a special ability to inspire others. After hearing her speak, young people went out to serve God in many places. She wrote many letters to friends and staff members. Her letters always included two things: "I am praying for you by name," and "Are you practicing rejoicing? Remember, the hard things make good rejoicing practice." (After while the staff called it GRP—Good Rejoicing Practice!)

Joy set the example as she continually rejoiced. She often said, "Rejoice now, right in the midst of this disappointment! God has something better. Don't wait to rejoice after God answers our prayer."

So when Joy discovered she needed to change the plans for traveling to Indonesia, she considered it an opportunity for good rejoicing practice. "God will work things out in His way," she said, and urged the staff to join in prayer with her.

Soon she declared, "We'll go by way of Australia instead of the way we'd planned."

A man named Stuart Mill met Joy and her two workers when they arrived in Australia. "I just recently heard about Gospel Recordings," he told Joy. He looked at this woman he had not met before. Her once-gray hair now looked nearly white. When she smiled, he wanted to smile, too.

"I'm awfully busy right now," he confessed, "but I've been asked to take you around while you're here." He noticed the pile of baggage beside Joy. "Uhh...you have quite a few things!"

Joy laughed. "Mr. Mill, these are the first portable tape recorders made by our staff. ReadyCorders, they're called. I had to bring along this conglomeration of things because we never know just what we'll need."

Joy opened her shoulder bag and let Stuart Mill look inside. Screwdrivers, little hammers, wire cutters, pliers, small bags of screws.... He couldn't begin to see everything!

It wasn't long until Stuart felt glad to be her chauffeur. "Joy," he said, "how wonderful it would be if we could have gospel records in all of the South Pacific dialects. There's a large empty room on the top floor of my factory. We could use it to store the records, and I would be willing to oversee getting them distributed."

"Oh, Stuart! That's what we've been praying for! I knew all along God would use our change in travel plans to bring something good." Joy beamed as she rejoiced in this new answer to prayer.

"If there's any other way I can help, let me know." Stuart added.

Without hesitating at all, Joy replied, "We need a record player with no parts to go wrong. It has to be something even a child from an uncivilized tribe can use without breaking it. The springs on our little wooden-box phonographs break easily. Stuart, I've been praying about this for years."

Sometime later, Stuart Mill used the idea God gave him to produce a motorless, hand-wind phonograph. They called the new machine a Phonette. Ten years after that he helped design something more simple—a record player made out of a piece of cardboard and a needle. Even the most primitive tribesperson could use this Card-Talk by turning the record with a stick.

*   *   *

One time Joy had to return to Los Angeles when she didn't want to go. "But we'll rejoice because God has something special for us," she said.

On that short stay at home she met Mr. Livingston Hogg, an electronics specialist from England. "I'm curious about Gospel Recordings," he told Joy.

Of course she was happy to explain about everything he wanted to know.

After Mr. Hogg returned home, he wrote an invitation to Joy. "Please stay with my wife and me when you come to England. We are interested in your work and I am sure others will be, also."

Joy did just that on her way to Africa. Mr. and Mrs. Hogg graciously welcomed her, saying, "We're planning a reception and you are to be the guest of honor."

"Oh my! That sounds so formal!" she exclaimed, surprised with this news. Then she thought, *What shall I wear?*

She remembered the small black hat she wore for most special occasions. She had gloves, too. But what about a suitable dress or suit? Then she smiled. *Yes, that special dress a friend gave to me! It'll be the proper thing to wear to an English reception. And I thought I'd never wear such a fancy dress! God always knows exactly what I need.*

Guests at the reception were glad to know about Joy's work. One of them—Gilbert Vinden—said afterward, "If there's any way my wife and I can help, we'll be ready."

It turned out God did have something for Mr. and Mrs. Vinden to do. They helped set up a Gospel Recordings distribution center in England.

* * *

By August of 1955, Joy had recorded languages in Africa for almost a year. Ann Sherwood and Sanna Barlow, another staff member, were with her.

Then they bought a new Willys jeep station wagon. "Isn't this wonderful?" asked Joy, looking pleased with the green vehicle that had KFA278 in big print on the license plate. "Now we can even go cross-country if we need to, whether the roads are good or not! We'll be able to find people we couldn't get to before."

And so the women set out in the jeep on an African safari into Tanganyika. Day by day they traveled among the light green and dark green trees and bushes, past Kilimanjaro, the highest mountain in Africa. As they went on, the landscape changed to dry brown. Only scrubby trees with rough tan bark sprouted up from sand and rocks.

Joy and her helpers stopped to record at mission centers along the way. Crowds of black-skinned Africans with hair shaved close often surrounded the jeep. Sometimes the vehicle even became their recording studio.

At the Kijota station, the recording team first heard about the Wakindiga tribe.

"They're little people, almost like pygmies," Howard Olson, the missionary, said. "They're small, but they have terrific muscles. They shoot bows that are seven feet high and their arrows never miss the mark! They're often hired to assist white men hunting elephants."

This information brought Joy to instant alertness. "What about their language?" she asked. "It must be different."

"Is it ever!" replied the missionary. "It's full of all kinds of weird clicks. No other African can understand them."

"Do you think we could get one of these people to make a recording for us?" Joy asked.

"I doubt it," Mr. Olson replied. "They're a dying-out tribe. Not many are left, although no one knows exactly how many there are. They're in the Yaida Swamps. But where? They're as unpredictable as the wild animals."

Joy had already made up her mind. "We must get this language, *by all means!*" she said. "It may be hard to locate them, but it's small isolated tribes like this who can be entirely missed unless they have the Gospel in their own language. We cannot leave these parts until we get this language!"

From that moment, Joy, Ann, and Sanna began to track down the Wakindiga. But how to communicate with these little people occupied their minds, too.

"It won't be impossible," said Joy. "God has always helped us before. He will this time, also."

The search for these people became a matter for special prayer. Meantime, Joy, Ann, and Sanna filled their days with making recordings of many other African languages. When they arrived at Iambi, they were close to the western border of the Yaida Swamp area.

"I'll send a runner to Isanzu," said Dean Peterson, the missionary at that station. "He can give the chief your request for Wakindiga people to come make recordings."

Joy prayed again, asking God to send the right people.

She and the others went on to the next mission station, Kinampanda. About the time they finished recording nine languages there, Howard Olson came with news. "The runner returned from Isanzu. He says the chief gave his word there'll be three Wakindiga to help you on Monday morning."

"Praise the Lord!" Joy shouted.

Early Monday morning, she and the others waited anxiously for missionary Bob Ward to arrive with the Wakindiga. At last he drove up. Three little bronze-brown men stepped out of the car, each carrying his long bow and arrow.

"This is the chief of the tribe!" said Bob Ward, pointing to the oldest Wakindiga man.

The Gospel Recordings team shrieked with delight.

For the next three days, the little men persevered. Simple sentence after simple sentence went from English to Swahili and Kinisanzu to the Kikindiga language.

"They catch our talk in a box," the African men said to one another. Later the chief remarked, "I'm teaching the box," and shook a crooked dark-brown finger at the mike.

The recording team patiently tested each sentence before going on to the next one. "We must be sure the meaning is clear," Joy explained to the missionaries.

It took several tries to get everything right.

At the end of the tedious work, Joy said to the men, "We want to come to your village."

"Night is coming," replied the little old chief whose bow stood taller than he did. "Our village is too far. It's too dangerous. There are wild animals."

"But we must come," Joy answered. "Where is it?"

The old man pointed across the canyon to a hill in the thorn-bush forest. He and his two tribesmen turned and were off to their camp, running as swiftly as wild deer.

Joy and her workers wasted no time in heading their jeep in the same direction. Bob Ward and another missionary named Edythe Kjellin went along, too. None of them could see any sign of a road as they jolted across sticks and stones and turned sharply to avoid stumps.

"I'm still thanking the Lord for this Willys jeep," said Joy. "We wouldn't be able to be out here without it."

Even before the missionaries reached the Wakindiga camp, the white people heard the joy-cry of the tribespeople. The little Africans, wearing scanty clothes, clambered over the rocks to greet the travelers, "Jambo, Mama! Jambo, Bwana!"

Presently the visitors sat down on flat rocks arranged like chairs under the giant baobab tree. Mud-and-straw huts, shaped like big beehives, clustered around on top of the dry, rocky ground. The little bush people murmured softly in the background. Four cooking fires sent up a warm red haze over the evening scene.

Bob Ward set the recorder gently on a low stone table. Inside the small machine were eight messages told in the clicks and clucks these people could understand. Each message lasted just three and a half minutes.

"The box learned the talk well," said the old chief. "The work was very big!"

Joy watched intently as the tribespeople listened to the story of God's love for the first time. She rejoiced because God had made it possible for these small forest-people to hear the Gospel in their own language.

* * *

In 1964, Joy and her staff celebrated 25 years of making gospel records.

"We have recorded 3,109 languages and dialects", she said. "Please ask God to bless the records—where they're made and where they're played. By themselves, the records are not powerful. They're useful only as God blesses each one."

Joy concluded by saying, "We can't quit yet! We must record more languages. Let's pray for others to help us."

The next year she declared, "It's time for us to go into Central America. We haven't had a recording team there yet."

Soon, she and two other workers started off on a journey that also took them into Mexico and South America.

Chapter 10

ONE LARGE GIFT

"How glad I am to be back," said Joy as she thrilled to the familiar sights and sounds and smells of Marcala, Honduras.

One evening, she attended a service in the little chapel. She delighted in discovering that many who came had become Christians while she was a missionary there.

On Sunday morning Joy and her companions traveled for three and a half hours over bad roads to a tiny village far back in the mountains. There she met a man who said, "I accepted Jesus as my Savior when you visited me in prison many years ago."

Joy remembered him. She smiled when he also said, "I have tried to be a witness. Now there are other believers, and we have built a small chapel."

She talked to several men in Tegucigalpa who had been her Bible school students in Marcala when they were young. Some of them had become the main preachers in Honduras.

As Joy and the others traveled on, someone told them, "You can't take your car across the border into Colombia unless you pay $2,000."

Joy gasped! "We don't have that much money! We must have the car, though, in order to do what we need to."

Joy telephoned her office in Los Angeles. Virginia Miller answered. "I'm glad you called. We've just received $2,000 someone gave as a personal gift to you. I didn't know how to get in contact with you."

Rejoicing came easy the rest of that day!

Once they were settled in a Colombian hotel, Joy noticed a few local townspeople waiting outside for a closer look at the Americans. She took advantage of the opportunity and brought out a Phonette and some Spanish gospel records.

The onlookers seemed fascinated with the music. A few lost interest and left when the spoken message started, but Rosalba stayed to listen all the way through.

She came back another time and waited to talk to Joy. "What does it mean to be a Christian?" Rosalba asked.

Joy was glad to tell her how she could be saved. They knelt together and Rosalba asked Jesus to be her Savior.

In a few days, Joy and the others drove to Cali. "I'm sorry to leave Rosalba and Don Luciano, the man she's living with," said Joy. "He's not ready to become a Christian yet. We must continue to pray for him even though we'll never see Rosalba again."

Joy didn't feel well for the next ten days after they reached Cali. She kept on anyway, not complaining as she wrote letters and made preparations for the rest of the trip.

Just before Christmas, Joy felt better. "Let's go to town," she said to her friend, Charlotte. "We'll buy a few little things and wrap them up as gifts for our neighbors."

Joy and Charlotte waded through the crowd of shoppers that flowed along like a river. Suddenly they heard, "Señorita Joy!" A happy-looking face pressed close to Joy.

"Rosalba!" Joy exclaimed. "I didn't expect to ever see you again. And especially not in this crowd. Why, we're more than 100 miles from where you live."

Don Luciano was standing with Rosalba. "We've come to visit my family," she told them.

Joy made plans to see Rosalba and Don Luciano another day. When that day came, however, Joy had to stay in bed again. She insisted the others go without her.

They came back with exciting news!

"Don Luciano accepted the Lord," they said. "And so did Rosalba's mother and sisters and her only brother."

Joy rejoiced. "And to think it all started with one little Spanish record!"

73

*   *   *

Encouraging letters continued to arrive at the office on Witmer Street. They all told about people who accepted Christ as Savior after hearing about Him on records made in their own languages. The staff rejoiced when they read such letters from Angola, Dutch New Guinea, Asia, Brazil, India, South America, Africa, and Algeria. Eskimos in Alaska had long ago worn out their first records.

One missionary wrote that after hearing the gospel records, people in his village said, "It is better than a fiesta! They make happiness in a town."

Two Garifuna boys in southern Belize shouted, "Hey, that's our language!" when they heard the voice from the Cardtalk. In another place a man told the missionary, "I knew the words were true because each time I listened, the little box said the same thing."

One letter had this to say: "We can't begin to count the number of people who have heard about the Lord Jesus for the first time in their lives because of the records you made for us." News came, also, about the Wakindiga who had become Christians.

Joy rejoiced, but quickly added, "This is not my doing. It's a matter of obediently walking through that door of service God promised He would open for me."

For over 45 years, Gospel records had sounded out from loudspeaker systems on rooftops, boats, or radio towers. Tribespeople and missionaries had played them on little phonographs carried up and down steep mountain trails. People had listened to them inside and outside, in all sorts of circumstances. Many of the recordings had also been transferred to cassette tapes.

Joy's childhood daydreams had never pictured anything like this. Still it was not enough!

"There's more yet to do!" Joy said emphatically.

Eventually the day came when she was too sick to take any more around-the-world trips, or even short trips. Most of the time she stayed in her two small rooms on Witmer Street.

As long as she was able, she wrote little notes and letters of encouragement. She prayed constantly and still had a strong desire for people everywhere to hear the Gospel in their own languages.

Other capable people took over when Joy could not direct Gospel Recordings any longer. They made sure the work continued.

Joy Ridderhof died on December 19, 1984. Many people came to honor her at the memorial service held in Los Angeles.

Dr. Robertson McQuilkin, whose father had so greatly influenced Joy, said at the service, "Joy was no ordinary person. She was one with joy-filled faith. She was a real pioneer because she did things others thought were impossible. She recorded more languages than some people said existed. She was instrumental in developing new ways of presenting the Gospel."

Everyone there remembered how Joy often encouraged them to pray, "Bless the records— where they're made and where they're played!"

The Columbia Bible College board of trustees chose to permanently remind others of what Joy had done with God's help. Shortly after her death, they announced a special honor for this early graduate of their school.

"The new Media and Music Center will be named the Joy Ridderhof Memorial Center. We hope many will follow her example of faith and trust in God."

Joy Ridderhof